Overcoming
Hardship

Conquering challenges
with determination

To Hana,
Keep shinning your light,
Loads of love,
Senada

SENADA DERVISEVIC

FIRST EDITION

ISBN: (paperback) 978-1-7397428-5-0

Overcoming Hardship by Senada Dervisevic is published by TC Publishing

For information please direct emails to: info@ibelieveican.co.uk

DEDICATION

In loving memory of my dear Mum

From a ZERO
I have become
My own HERO

CONTENTS

INTRODUCTION

Life is full of surprises. You never know what will happen or what obstacles life will set in your path. Life has hit me hard. But I hit back harder. I survived each event and came out stronger and more determined than before.

The problem today is that some people do know how to take the first step to begin overcoming hardship .

The severity of their struggles can paralyse them and that makes the problem worse .

I wrote this book to help the many people who asked for my assistance in overcoming their hardships. The steps I describe in this book are the same ones that I applied to my life and I pray that they can help you too.

CHAPTER ONE

I AM A SURVIVOR

Here I am despite it all

Life was beautiful before all the chaos began in 1992. My parents gave me and my siblings everything that we could wish for. My father, grandpa, and uncles ran a construction business together. My mother was a homemaker. We were a close-knit family living the good life in the suburbs. I remember having all my uncles, aunties, and cousins around me regularly and that was thanks mostly to the role that my mother played.

Bosnia is a beautiful country where I like to go and spend my holidays with my daughter. People are so nice and you're also always welcome there no matter who you are or where you come from. Bosnians are always happy to help others and welcome visitors to the beautiful country of Bosnia and Herzegovina.

My mother belonged to a wealthy and well-respected family and she was a powerful personality. She was the glue that kept our nuclear family and extended family together. As the youngest child, I spent most of my time with her and I learned to be the person I am today because of what she taught me. She taught all of her children how to treat people with respect and equality, no matter their colour or religion. She never hesitated to go out of her way to help someone. Women in Bosnia had very limited rights in the eighties and nineties but she did what she could to empower them and help them.

I was nine years old when it all started. I was playing outside my school with several other children when our families came rushing in to collect us. The army had surrounded the city and was in the process of occupying it. It was a terrifying sight for a child so young. One minute we were living a happy peaceful life. The next, it was total devastation. Our once-peaceful existence changed overnight into one of fear and terror. Everyday tasks like going to school, the market, or the bank became impossible. Access to food was limited, and people hid in their homes because the alternative was facing the guns and brutality of the soldiers in the streets.

When Bosnia was besieged, my father and uncles were away working in Slovenia. My older sister was married and living with her in-laws in the same city but she was far enough away that it was not possible for us to go there or for her to come to us once the war began. So it was just me, my brother, and my mother.

The war in Bosnia and Herzegovina came about as a result of break-up of the socialist Federal Republic of

Yugoslavia thanks to the weakening the of the confederate system that was in place at the end of the Cold War.

The country of Bosnia and Herzegovina consists of three main ethnic groups - Bosniaks, Serbs, and Croats. All three groups are seen as equal in the county's constitution and none is considered a minority. But that doesn't stop people from disliking other groups.

The leader of the Serbs took advantage of ethnic tensions caused by the war, looking to exterminate Bosniaks and take over our territory.

Initially, we were able to shelter in place because my mother, being the resourceful person that she was, had stocked enough supplies to last us for a few months. Our displaced neighbours moved in and contributed what they could. With the help of our neighbours, she would combine resources and make sure everyone was fed and had shelter. The neighbours would make loaves of bread and other items that would be easy to store or give away to those in need.

Outside, right in front of our eyes, people were being raped and killed. Soldiers were scattered everywhere. The sounds of gunfire and bombs were a constant assault on our senses. At night the soldiers would bang on the doors of the houses at random. Sometimes they would demand money or jewellery. Sometimes they would be looking for boys and young men to capture and imprison. Sometimes they would pull out the women and brutalise them.

Tragedy struck one night when soldiers raided my granddad's house. They demanded all the money, valuables, and jewellery in the house. He did not have much money on him since banks were not operating during the war. He was rounded up along with hundreds of others. We did not hear what happened to him until many years later.

My mum was a really brave woman. After learning about the way her father had been taken by the soldiers, she was more determined to help as many people as she could. She let many of the displaced people in our neighbourhood stay at our house. There were so many people, I couldn't count them all. My mum didn't care; she just wanted to make sure everyone was safe.

We happened to have a secret basement that my dad built beneath the kitchen. He probably meant it to be a storage area for my mum, but it was a Godsend because we used it to hide my brother, who was fourteen at the time, and the other males from the neighbourhood, who my mother was helping. The scariest thing was that the army had taken over a house opposite ours and was using it as a barrack. So it was essential to stay out of their sight. We were unable to go out and play or do any outdoor activity.

But one day we were told to evacuate our homes. Those who refused would be shot immediately. The women were threatened with rape. We had fifteen minutes in which to gather our belongings and escape.

We had to flee from our homes with whatever essentials we could grab. We didn't have time to contact anyone. We had to run for our lives.

We escaped to a nearby forest and spent around a week in hiding. It was a long walk to the forest and we were exhausted, cold, and hungry. There were not enough blankets and we could not make fires to keep warm.

Food was limited, but my mother helped to organise whatever edibles were available and made sure that at least the children and as many other people as possible were fed. Even then, many went hungry. We had no water with which to wash or clean ourselves. The sounds of bombs and gunfire followed us into the forest.

A week later, the soldiers made announcements for people to return to their homes. We had no idea what state our homes were in. The walk back was a nightmare for me. At nine years old it was traumatic to witness the death and destruction all around me. People who refused to leave their homes were brutally tortured and killed. Their bodies were left out in the streets. Many of the areas were bombed and body parts were strewn everywhere. I remember that the adults organised the collection of the dead and gathered their parts for burial. Now I am thankful that I was able to escape their fate and feel at peace that I had the chance to help put their bodies at rest.

When we arrived back home we had to put a white flag in the window. This was a sign to show that people lived in the house and would not cause any damage. But the soldiers could do damage to anyone living in the houses. They were in charge and there was nothing we could do to stop them.

CHAPTER TWO

THE GREAT ESCAPE

Too determined to be defeated

The place we lived in was at the centre of the war. Our hometown had become very unsafe and it was no longer possible for us to stay there. A collective decision was made by all the members of our neighbourhood to move to the nearest safe town. We set out early in the morning and joined thousands of people who seemed to have the same idea as us. For the entire journey, I remember being in constant fear. Scores of troops marched alongside us. Many called us horrible names. They grabbed people at random from the travelling groups to harass, rob, or simply to exterminate. It was a long and terrifying walk that took us the whole day and I remember that it was getting dark when we arrived.

People from all over Bosnia had made their way to this town that had somehow been spared from the worst of this war, and I am sure that we were all thankful for it. The locals helped us settle into temporary shelters and provided us with whatever food and clothing that they could spare.

We spent several weeks here, crowding together in apartment buildings, sleeping on the floor. Some people were familiar to us but most were strangers. We waited for other friends and family members, especially my sister and my granddad, to join us. We could only pray for their safety as there was no way to contact them.

Due to the shortage of food, meat and vegetables were unavailable so the only thing we had to eat was plain, boiled white rice. It sustained us for all the weeks that we stayed in that town. As a result, the sight of rice makes me nauseated to this day.

Eventually, aid workers from all over the world began to arrive to help the Bosnian survivors. They registered us and we gave them whatever information we had for family members outside of Bosnia. One of my aunts was living in Croatia and my dad was still in Slovenia. We were able to contact them through the aid workers and at the first opportunity, we managed to flee Bosnia. My mum, brother, and I were first bundled into a truck and then onto a bus and taken to Croatia. My father was already waiting for us when we arrived in Croatia and we lived with my aunt until other arrangements could be made.

My sister was still stuck in Bosnia. We managed to get in touch with her and tell her where we were. Nine months later she, her husband, and her in-laws were able to join us in Croatia. Her husband and his uncles had all been prisoners in a camp where they were starved and tortured. Fortunately, they were released and that is when she made her way to Croatia with the rest of her family. It was a bittersweet reunion with many tears and much laughter.

After a few years in Croatia, she and her family moved to the UK. We were never able to make contact with my grandfather.

My father's job continued in Slovenia and he provided for us however he could. My brother and I began attending school in Croatia and slowly but surely, we started our new life.

Seven years later, with the war finally over, my mom decided she wanted to go back to Bosnia. Being a builder and architect, it was easy for my dad to begin rebuilding our house.

Two years after we moved back to Bosnia we received news about the horrible fate of my granddad. We discovered that after he was taken from his home the night of the occupation, all the prisoners were taken to the school I used to attend before the war. He was one among hundreds that were massacred in this senseless war in Bosnia.

During the war, those who were killed could not be identified and did not receive proper burials. The bodies were just dumped in mass graves on a wasteland. Once the war was over, the authorities attempted to make identifications and hand over the remains to their families.

Nine years after his death, my mum was asked to identify her dad's body. This affected my mum terribly. When she came home after making the identification, she was very quiet. She didn't say much and continued with her routine tasks around the house. A memorial service was held for my grandfather and the 200 men who were executed alongside him once all the bodies were identified.

Not long after this, my brother and I arrived home from school one day. Mum was in the kitchen setting out lunch and we joined her at the dining table. As we ate our food we noticed that she didn't look well. Something was seriously wrong with her. She needed help.

If we had called the ambulance, it would have taken them too long to get there since the medical services infrastructure had still not recovered from the war. Though the war had ended a while ago, many services were still not operating at full strength. We called the neighbours, who offered to take my mum and my brother to the hospital.

My brother took mum in his arms and helped to put her in the back of the car. The neighbour drove them to the hospital. I stayed with another of our neighbours as my brother felt that I was too young to accompany him. At the time I was angry with them for leaving me behind.

But today I know that my brother was only trying to protect me. He understood that I would never recover if I had watched my mother leave this world.

Hours passed before they returned, without my mother. I kept asking them, "Where is Mum? Why is she not back?" They told me she didn't make it to the hospital. My mum had had a stroke and passed away in my brother's arms. I let out an almighty scream. It was so loud that the neighbours came running. I was in shock; I couldn't believe that my hero had left me alone in this world at only fifteen years old.

The neighbours were very supportive. Whatever we needed, they were there to provide us with it. Much of their kindness was due to the respect and love that they had for my mother. The funeral was arranged by my family. The service was attended by family members near and far – many of my uncles and other relatives from around the world, my sister and her children all came to pay respect to Mummy. It was hard for her too, as she had been living in the UK and hadn't seen us for a few years.

Once we put my mum to rest, it was time for my life to change once again. My father had to return to work in Slovenia. My brother was older now and going to university. So, I had to decide what I wanted to do with my life.

I had two options: I could go with my father to Slovenia, or move to the UK and live with my sister, as she had no blood relatives there. I decided to move to the UK as I would have access to better resources and opportunities to better myself in the UK.

Arriving in the UK

It was cold, wet, and rainy. I arrived in a foreign country, all on my own, with a single pink suitcase. I was only fifteen and in my short life, I had to flee from war and rebuild a life in Croatia; I lost my mum and then was told that I had to start a new life by myself. I was still grieving. I lost my hero when I needed her the most. I kept asking, why is this happening to me? Why did she leave me? How am I going to get by?

But then I remembered how strong she was and I made a decision to take strength from my mother's memory and be as brave and focused as she was in her life.

I did not speak a word of English and I was not entitled to any benefits as I was not a citizen. My sister had signed a form to say she was going to finance me whilst I was in the UK, which was one of the reasons I was able to get there.

I was determined to learn how to speak English so I enrolled in an ESOL course (English for Speakers of Other Languages), and within six months I accomplished my goal. The ESOL teachers were amazing and I would take any English book from the library and read whatever I could. If I did not understand a word, I used a Bosnian-English dictionary to decipher its meaning, and wherever I went I would use my book to communicate with people.

The following year I enrolled for my A-Levels and passed with flying colours. I got my first job in a well-known biscuit store where I worked evenings and attended college during the day. A teacher in my college encouraged me to apply to university, which I did. Every application was successful – I had my pick of higher learning institutions. But due to a technical issue, I was classed as an international student and would have to pay a staggering £9,000 for my course. I was extremely upset because I did not have that kind of money.

Instead of falling into despair, though, I thought to myself, "What can I do to help myself succeed? There must be another way." I did my research and found out about an Open University. I applied and got in. I worked hard and passed my Social Science course.

This opened the door for me to get a job at a dental surgery. Initially, I worked at the reception and did administrative work, but my manager saw my interest in dental surgery and encouraged me to apply for dental nursing training.

Once again technicalities became obstacles and I was told to re-do my GCSEs because they were outdated for the course I wanted to attend. The manager promised that if I achieved good grades in my GCSEs, they would finance the rest of my education. And so that is what I did. I never had any issues with studying hard and getting good grades. Off I went and studied at Bradford College and Leeds University Hospital. I have been in my job in the medical field for the last fifteen years and I absolutely love the work.

This is the foundation for my story. Along my journey, I have learned many lessons that I will share with you in the coming chapters; all the skills I learned to help me overcome the many hardships I faced.

CHAPTER THREE

CHANGE YOUR THINKING

Positive thinking, positive outcome

You will experience hardships, but the outcome depends on how you choose to overcome them. Do you just sit and cry? Or do you decide to do something about it? Yes, cry if you have to. But try to get up and take those first baby steps even if you do so with tears falling down your cheeks. If I can do it, you can too. There is nothing in this world that you can't survive, so keep going. You will get through these tough times.

Your mind is occupied with positive and negative thoughts and you have to decide how you will deal with the challenges you face.

You have to make a daily decision to focus on the positive. Think about the things and people that you have in your life. The moment you think in this way, your life changes.

Positive thoughts, positive mind

This can seem impossible when you feel depressed. But learning how to challenge those negative thoughts can be life-changing. Life challenges us all. It can bring you to your knees. During these times of testing, you will face many trials. Life will change suddenly. But remember that your situation, whether good or bad, is only temporary.

When I found life challenging, I found that I was looking at everything negatively. And I realised that I had to change the way I was thinking.

> **"After every difficulty
> comes ease"**

God is a very important aspect of my life. When I am stressed, going for a walk or run gives me positive energy and makes me happy. So my advice is to never lose hope.

My faith and trust in God helped me through all the times when I was struggling. I experienced many sleepless nights. But I prayed day and night for God to give me courage, strength, and patience. I knew good times would return.

"Show your attitude with gratitude"

What are you grateful for? Is it the people who supported you through your hardships? Are you grateful for what God has already given you? Or what you have already achieved in your life? It's important to acknowledge the good things in your life. The more you focus on the positive, the more good you will see.

I am grateful to God for all my hardships because those hardships made me stronger, and helped me become the person I am today. I am achieving all my goals and succeeding more in my life journey now. So I am very proud of myself and all I have achieved because I trusted God to keep me in His protection. I always say, show your attitude with gratitude. Having gratitude will help you stay motivated and keep you going no matter how hard life is.

I find journaling helps me to stay focused, and maintain a positive frame of mind. When I write down each day what I am grateful for, I feel more positive and successful. In this way, I am showing how grateful I am. I am grateful to God to be alive, and for what I have achieved so far. I thank God for everything I have in my life.

Thinking more positively has changed my life and outlook. A song that comes to mind is 'Brand-new me' by Alicia Keys. I now have a brand-new me and a brand-new life. I have learned to say no to people if what they are asking is not in alignment with my values.

Do not let your mind be drowned in negative thoughts. They can randomly pop into your head and the more you try to control them, the more they occupy your mind. This is a definition of faulty thinking. You know that this kind of thinking is wrong. And even though you may not be able to stop these thoughts, you can control whether or not you dwell on them. You need to identify that the thought is not fruitful and stop it in its tracks. It may be hard to do, especially in the beginning, but the more you practice, the easier it gets to banish negative thoughts before they take hold of you and discover a better version of yourself.

Set your goals

Set yourself some realistic goals. What do you want to achieve? A goal without any action is just a dream. To succeed in life, it is very important to plan and act purposefully to achieve your goals.

For example, I write down all my goals before I go to bed. When I wake up the next morning, I check my journal and see what I have written down as my first goal for that day. I start straight away and take action to accomplish this first goal.

To make your dreams come true, you need to take action now. Even if the first action is small and doesn't seem like it will matter, remember that many small actions add up to a significant action. If the first step is too much for you, break that step down into smaller, manageable steps and begin the journey to your dream.

> **"If you believe,
> you will achieve"**

I made a conscious decision to change myself. I decided that I needed to set goals and, most importantly, set a time limit on achieving those goals.

For example, I joined an authors' lab – a 90-day writing programme. Our coach set us a time limit which kicked us into action. It forced me to work hard. If a deadline had not been set, I would have taken my time, or even lost my motivation and then stopped working on my goals. If you don't take any action, it will be a long time before you see your dream come true. Don't quit on your dreams. Keep going.

CHAPTER FOUR

DON'T GIVE UP

After every difficulty, comes ease

There was a point in my life when I was struggling with many things at once. My relationship with my spouse was breaking down, my family was pressuring me to patch things up with him and that made my depression and anxiety spiral out of control. Then came my health issues, which made things even worse.

The diagnosis

I was experiencing persistent infections and had to go through some extensive diagnostics. I remember when my doctor told me that he suspected I have cancer and that I could be dying. That was very difficult to hear and deal with, and when I heard the news I felt so overwhelmed. All I wanted was for it to stop.

I was by myself, and all I did was cry day and night as I could not see a way out. My family tried to support me through phone calls as they were still in Bosnia and I had no support from my husband. I was only thinking about my daughter and what she would do without me if I died. Day and night I prayed to God, "Please make me better, my daughter needs me."

The words 'don't quit' kept ringing in my ears. I realised that quitting life is never an option. That made me fight and I knew that if I wanted to get back to good health, I needed to draw on my inner strength to make it through. I needed to be strong to overcome my current test.

I told the doctor that my faith in God was stronger than his words. I knew I would get through this. God would help me. So I put all my energy into getting better. I went for all the treatments and scans that the doctors recommended, and I focused on healing my illness and beating cancer. I was grateful that the doctors had caught it in time or it may have been too late for me to recover.

I talked to God constantly and I communicated with my daughter. They gave me the strength I needed because I knew that I had to make it through for my princess. I also had the time to reflect on all the negative aspects of my life and analyse what changes I needed to make.

It took a few months before I was declared cancer-free. I was still very weak but I decided to take baby steps and take care of myself. Each day I got a little better and my energy started to come back. Also, my confidence began to soar as my vision for my future became clearer.

Faith in God

My faith in God was stronger than ever and to this day I always thank Him for everything. God has never let me down and every hardship I have faced has made me stronger.

> **"God will make a way where there seems to be no way"**

My Turning Point

After my battle with cancer, I came to the conclusion that life is too short and precious to waste. I needed to forget the past and live in the present. If you think too much about the past, depression and anxiety become your constant companions. And the way they affect your physical and mental health is just not beneficial to anyone, especially yourself. Don't waste precious time. Live in the moment. Live your best life.

Positive mindset

Stop worrying about and overthinking everything. Every problem has a solution. Take action; you have to plan and set your goals to achieve them. Nothing comes easy in life. You have to work very hard to succeed. Trust the process and you will get there.

Life is a journey that goes up and down but you are the one who chooses the direction of your life. Enjoy your life and don't waste time, because you don't know if you're going to see the next day. You can turn everything around when you think positively while facing hardships. It is important to deal with what you are going through.

Before my diagnosis, there were times when I would sit alone at night with a lit candle and a cup of coffee. My mind would be racing with thoughts. I had decided to lock myself in my own little world. My mind was all over the place, rambling into places where it should not. I tried to stop it but I could not. My internal pain and my inner struggles were only known to me because I was experiencing them.

People would say there is a light at the end of the tunnel. But I kept asking myself, when will that light appear? How long does it take to get to the end of this tunnel? I felt that the people telling me to move on or get a grip did not understand what I was feeling. They were not wrong, because change only happens when you start to believe in it. Locking myself away was not the answer, I know that now.

My favourite quote which my powerful mum taught me is:

**"Stand by truth even if you
need to walk alone"**

Once I had won my battle with cancer, I knew I had to make the changes needed to get my life back on track. For me to move forward, I had to believe that I could do it. I had to believe in myself. So that's what I did. That process was extremely difficult and stressful, but I refused to give up. I kept going. I had a reason to live. I had a beautiful daughter and she needed me. I told myself, "I am strong. I am smart. I am enough".

**"When life hits you,
you hit harder"**

Life may knock you over, but you can't let it keep you down. You have to get up. You have to fight back against the circumstances that put you on the ground. It's not easy, but the hard work always pays off in the end. When you achieve your goals, you become happy and successful again.

Healing

Healing takes time. It is a long process and it doesn't happen overnight. The process you have to go through to heal and move in a positive direction is long and tedious. It involves adopting new, good habits and breaking old, bad habits; making and adapting to major life changes; identifying and getting rid of toxic relationships; or overcoming the grief of losing the things and people that we love the most.

You need to allow yourself enough time to heal when you are going through pain. Because once you heal and the pain goes away, you can look at life again and move on in a more positive direction. It doesn't matter how long it takes, as long as you heal in the end.

When you are healing, you go through the emotional state of asking yourself why this happened to you, why you allowed it to happen, and wondering when you will feel better. It is an essential process that helps you learn from your poor decisions. But you must not allow yourself to dwell on it for too long, other than to analyse it.

Once you heal, you can build a better version of yourself because you can learn so much from your mistakes and the things that you let go of. You become a stronger version of yourself that can achieve anything in life that you set your mind to.

CHAPTER FIVE

BELIEVE IN YOURSELF

Setting yourself up for success

To heal and start my new life, I had to stay away from negative, toxic people. I have encountered some people who were negative and didn't understand my pursuit to keep bettering myself. They didn't think I would achieve anything.

Removing negativity and toxicity from your life begins with those who are the closest to you. It may be a close relative, a spouse, a sibling, or quite possibly even a child. For me, it was my husband of fifteen years.

I married young and had a daughter five years later. As with every couple, we had our ups and downs. We tried to work through them as they came. But sometimes you need to analyse if the person you are investing all your time, energy, and effort into is worth it. Is it worth waiting for them to make the same effort as you? To fight as hard as you, to fix what is broken? Or is it truly the time to let go and allow yourself to breathe and heal? I decided that it wasn't worth waiting and hoping for him to change. We got a divorce and went our separate ways.

Believing in yourself also means you must hold yourself accountable for the role you play in your relationships. Nothing is ever one-sided as it takes two hands to clap. Be honest and avoid the blame game. Once you have a clear picture you can make a better, more beneficial decision without any regrets.

Life can be challenging, and you can lose faith in yourself. You may wonder if life will ever get better. Life will always happen, unplanned and unexpected. But how you manage life when things do not go your way is the key. My faith in God has helped me through everything that could overwhelm me. And you can achieve anything if you put your mind to it.

If you don't believe in yourself, you will find it hard to succeed. Be real with yourself. Acknowledge that you are going through a difficult time.

But remember you will get through it.

**"I believe I can,
and I know I will"**

Believing in myself has been my biggest life lesson. By taking small steps each day you will build back your confidence and start believing in yourself again. When you start believing in yourself, there is nothing in this world that you cannot achieve. Decide today that you will trust yourself and the process. Everything takes time. Changes are not made overnight.

You are the one who decides which way you want to go. Whether you want to stay in pain or decide to work towards healing so that you can move on with your life. It is never too late to start a better life.

> **"After every difficulty,
> comes ease"**

After the rain, the sun always comes out and shines again. It is the same with your life. Look at life from the positive side and positive things will start to happen again. Have faith in yourself and you will see the difference. It is important to take breaks, rest and gather your strength. But you cannot give up. No matter how hard life gets. Accept yourself with all the good and the bad. Focus on fixing the bad and improving the good within you, and stop comparing yourself to others. Always say to yourself:

> **"I am enough, I am strong,
> and I am unstoppable"**

Repeat the above quote to yourself each day and you will start to see the difference in yourself.

I remember when I was going through an extremely difficult time in my marriage. My whole world had come crashing down. I felt lost and shattered. I felt abandoned. Everything at the time just seemed impossible. I was in a negative state of mind and I didn't see a way out of my situation. I cried day and night, and became depressed and anxious about everything. I didn't know which way to go or how to resolve that situation. It was extremely painful and I felt paralysed.

When facing such a difficult situation, you may find yourself asking, "why?" over and over in your head. Why is this happening to me? Do I deserve this? I questioned myself so much until one day I woke up and said to myself, "Get up now, there is so much more to your life. You can do this." It was not easy, but I know I had to do it because no one could do it for me.

Nothing comes easy. No major change happens overnight. You will achieve your dreams. But it all starts with you and changing the way you think.

**"She believed she
could, so she did"**

CHAPTER SIX

SELF-CARE

I am important

Self-love and self-care are very important. Getting enough sleep, exercising, and eating healthy are not just current trends. They do make you feel better. You know when you are sick, physically, mentally, emotionally, or spiritually. And over time, it all heals as you put in the work, make the right choices, to get better. All the parts contribute to your well-being.

. . . .
"Self-care is not being selfish"
. . . .

We all need to look after ourselves. If we are not feeling good, how can we help ourselves or help others? Looking after ourselves is essential. The first thing we need to do is get up from that couch and take action. We also need to change our negative thoughts.

Exercise

Exercise is an important part of your physical and mental health. The benefits of exercising include feeling more active and healthy, and the hormones released due to exercise make us feel happier. The more you exercise, the better you feel. Your health improves and you can see life more positively. It is easier to believe that you can't achieve anything, but this is not true.

On my healing journey, my inner voice kept telling me to get up from that couch and take action now. Those words hit me hard, and I acknowledged that I needed to take better care of myself. I was neglecting my physical health. I wasn't eating the right foods, I was staying in bed, and not taking care of myself. So I made it a point to take up some physical activity like walking or running.

Mental health

As important as physical health is, mental health cannot be overlooked. Your state of mind is important. You need to change your unhelpful thinking style and focus on thinking positively. Hardship impacts your health, both physically and mentally. Many people know how to look after their physical health, which offers many tangible signs of need, but fail to understand how to take care of their mental health because ill health here isn't something you can see or touch.

When you are overwhelmed by the circumstances around you, sometimes you cannot think straight. You are constantly battling with negative thoughts, maybe even suicidal ones, and you cannot concentrate or think clearly about what is happening around you or do any productive work.

I have learned through my life experiences, especially during COVID and my battle with cancer, that health is a crucial aspect of life. When we are healthy we can achieve more of the goals that we set for ourselves, and we can also help others achieve their goals too.

How to change your unhelpful thinking:

#1 Change your mindset
   With positive thinking, you will have a positive outcome.
#2 Start believing in yourself even when no one else is
#3 Set your goals and take action today in order to succeed in your life

If you believe it, you will achieve it.

- Stay positive.
- Stay blessed.
- Stay focused.
- Let the God do the rest.

Supportive People

Surround yourself with like-minded people because you will always get the support you need. People who believe in you and support you are the key to overcoming hardship. It does not have to be a massive network of family and friends. It can be a handful of trusted individuals or a non-judgmental support group that will support you through your time of need. Someone you can talk to, who understands your perspective and advise you without bias.

On my journey, I have met some amazing people. When I felt stuck, being around like-minded people helped me get unstuck.

As I said before, being around people who are toxic or negative is not going to benefit you. Surround yourself only with people of quality and those who you can learn from. They will help you to achieve your goals and dreams. Have people in your life who will treat you with respect, dignity, love, kindness, and loyalty. People you can call on when you need them. They will help to create and maintain a positive environment in which you all can thrive together.

Meditate

Meditation is very important for our mental health. When we feel depressed and anxious, meditating helps to ease these negative emotions. That is why many people choose to meditate. I love to meditate because it helps me navigate through my negative thoughts and replace them with positive ones. The benefit of meditation is that it can help reduce anxiety and improve your mood. Positive mental health is good for you and it makes you feel good.

Prayer

Praying is a very important aspect of my life. I start my day by praying. I believe in God and I believe that God always helps me when I cannot find a way out of my difficult situations. He shows me how to overcome each hardship. God is always there for me. People may come and go but God is always there. I always thank God for everything. The benefit of praying for me is that I feel the joy in my life again when I make a connection with God through prayer.

Prayer can help you to start believing in yourself again. In prayer, you can find your inner peace and happiness once again. Praying gives you hope and helps you to think positively about yourself, others around you, and things that are happening in your life.

> **"The best investment is an investment in ourselves"**

Looking after your health is important. All things are possible if you believe. It takes courage to be different. I have also learned that little things can make you happy. You don't need to be rich to be happy. I always say to my family and friends, "Don't spend too much money on me, money does not make me happy. Even if you buy me a candle, I am happy."

CHAPTER SEVEN

MAKE THE IMPOSSIBLE POSSIBLE

Get off the couch and take action

The motto that I live by is:

> **"Get up from that couch and take action if you want to succeed"**

I began my journey toward a better life by seeking help from my life coach (and now my publisher) Tarnya Coley. I set out my goals by using plans and strategies in her book *Plan it, See it, Anticipate it*, which is also her go-to advice for a better life

I always say, "If you believe it, you will achieve it."

The first thing I did was to grab a pen and write down my goals. Once I put all my goals down on paper, I decided which ones were on my priority list. Then I planned out the steps that would help me achieve my goals. I anticipated my goals and then I took action to make sure that I achieved each and every one of them.

Discipline

You have to be very disciplined, focused, positive and full of self-belief as you work towards achieving a goal. Everything is possible and you can make the impossible possible, but you have to get up and take that first step.

It's not enough to just have a plan and strategies. You must take action. If you do not take action you will not be able to achieve anything. I know first-hand that when it is time to make important decisions to bring your life into order, it can be scary. I am more than aware of how much fear, anxiety, and negativity it can stir up. But you have to break through that fear and to face the things that seem difficult to achieve your goals and dreams.

As I always say, "If you believe, you will achieve. To achieve each goal, you have to take one step at a time. Taking action, step by step, you will be able to achieve all your goals and dreams, because dreams do come true if you work hard for them. Hard work always pays off.

You have to gain more knowledge and more practice to present yourself and your knowledge to the whole world. A positive mindset is very important. When you get tired it is important to rest your mind. Only then can you reflect on the best course of action to take.

When you think of the possibilities, everything around you becomes easier. But if you think negatively, everything around you becomes negative. So always reflect and set your mind towards a positive direction. Think positive and then you will see positive results in every aspect of your life.

> "Allow yourself time to achieve your goals. Succeed in making the impossible, possible."

That is how I started. The most important thing is to believe in yourself, set that goal and believe that you will achieve it. Some of my favourite motivational mantras that encourage me to keep going are:

> "Don't stop. Never give up"
> "Quitting is never an option"
> "I am strong, I am smart, and I am enough"

These words help me to stay focused, continue to take action, and trust the process during hardships.

You always have a choice. Everything depends on how you decide to deal with each situation and which way you decide to go. You have to be responsible for your actions and you need to have the grace and wisdom to realise that you may fail. It is easier to give up and not face that reality. But, as I have said before, quitting is never an option.

> **"There's no shame in falling down! True shame is to not stand up again!"**
> - Midorima Shintarō

There is no shame in admitting failure or defeat because you can always start all over again. This is essential to overcoming hardships in your life. Big or small, face the reality of the situation, and be brave and strong. If you don't try something new you will never be able to learn from your mistakes and grow into a new and better you. Keep trying, no matter what, because one day you will achieve and succeed more than you could have ever imagined.

I knew that I had to go through the painful process of eliminating the negative and toxic elements in my life to obtain something better. I want to point out that my faith in God is very important and that all the days and nights I spent praying for help and guidance helped me to overcome hardships. If you have a strong faith in God then you will more easily overcome hardships. God never leaves you alone. God is always there for you. God will make a way, even ife there seems no way.

My prayer

Dear God thank you for everything.
I will always stay positive.
I am blessed.
I will stay focused.
I will do my best
And let you, O' God, do the rest.

So believe in yourself, make your plans, set your goals, put in the hard work, don't lose faith, don't give up, and trust that God has made the best plans for you. If I can do it you can do it too.

CHAPTER EIGHT

TAKE SMALL STEPS

Small steps add up to big results

When you feel depressed and anxious, everything becomes difficult. Even getting out of bed. You could even become bed-bound. You can't imagine brushing your hair or your teeth. It will seem to be the most difficult thing in the world for you to do, but this is the point where is it important to take action. It is the absolute right time to take that first baby step.

I know it is not easy, but as soon as you take that first step it will be easier to take another step and then the next one. Each step after that will get easier and easier to make because you will begin to find your inner strength and motivation. Because the truth is that hardships make you stronger and better.

I work with people suffering with poor mental health. I have been there and I know you have to keep on going no matter how hard life seems at that particular moment. You have to take those first steps and put in the hard work to make a better life for yourself. To become your own success story.

Support from others can help you through this time. If you need someone to motivate you, someone to poke, prod, push and even shove you if necessary, find your person or people and use every resource at your disposal. The hurdle may seem huge at first, but every little step that you take brings you closer to getting over that hurdle and reaching the other side.

We need to keep reminding ourselves that nothing comes easy in life. Everything takes time and a lot of effort to achieve, especially something good for you. Take action by planning and anticipating your next steps to overcome hardships and achieve your next goal.

Remember:

Positive thoughts = positive results.
Negative thoughts = negative results.

It's very important to control your thoughts to have a happy life.

If you believe in yourself, you can achieve everything you set your mind to.

- Work hard
- Stay positive
- Stay focused
- And let God do the rest

So, to recap, here are the points to focus on as you set out on your journey towards overcoming your hardships and creating a better, stronger version of yourself and your life:

- Believe in yourself
- Accept that things need to change
- Think positive
- Remove the negative
- Keep your faith in God, trust His plan for you
- Take care of yourself in every way
- Surround yourself with supportive people
- Don't quit, don't give up
- Don't be afraid to fail
- Plan your priorities
- Take small steps

Reach out to me if you need support through your journey. May God be with you every step of the way.

LAST WORD

Be strong enough to let go and
wise enough to wait for what you deserve.

RECOMMENDED BOOKS THAT HELPED ME

The love of God
- *Audrey McFarlane*

Plan it. See it. Anticipate it
- *Tarnya Coley*

The woman of Paradise
- *Muhammad Irshad Qasmi*

REVIEW ASK

Thank you for reading this book. If you found this book useful, please consider leaving a short review on Amazon to help other readers know what the book is about and how it can help them.

Follow Senada Dervisevic on:

Facebook:

https://www.facebook.com/senada.dervisevichalilovic

ABOUT THE AUTHOR

Senada loves writing and always has a journal to express herself through writing. Senada writes because she loves to share her knowledge with the world, inspiring hope and motivating others. Her mission is to serve women, to help them know that they can overcome life's challenges and achieve their goals and dreams.

Senada resides in the UK with her beautiful daughter. She loves reading nonfiction books about personal development, health and wellness, entrepreneurship, and mindset while helping women to overcome hardships.